D1117462

MANPOWER
FOR
MILITARY
MOBILIZATION

MANPOWER FOR MILITARY MOBILIZATION

Kenneth J. Coffey

American Enterprise Institute for Public Policy Research
Washington, D.C.

Kenneth J. Coffey is a military manpower consultant to the Department of Defense, the Congressional Budget Office, and other government agencies.

Library of Congress Cataloging in Publication Data

Coffey, Kenneth J
    Manpower for military mobilization.

    (AEI studies ; 189)
    1. Manpower—United States. 2. United States.
Army—Reserves. 3. United States. Army—Mobilization.
4. Military Service, Compulsory—United States.
I. American Enterprise Institute for Public Policy
Research. II. Title. III. Series: American Enterprise Institute
for Public Policy Research. AEI studies ; 189.
UA17.5.U5C59   355.2′2′0973   78-6618

ISBN 0-8447-3291-5

Printed in the United States of America

CONTENTS

INTRODUCTION

The capability of the U.S. Army to respond to the challenges of a major conventional confrontation in Europe between the forces of NATO and of the Warsaw Pact has been significantly reduced as a result of the decision to adopt an All-Volunteer Force (AVF). Indeed, unless corrective actions are taken, by 1980 more than a third of the army's reserve forces personnel needed to augment the active army upon mobilization will not be available. This shortfall would represent fully a quarter of the army's current requirement of manpower for mobilization.

Reliance on the army's reserve forces (the Army National Guard and the Army Reserve) for most of the manpower needed is a basic tenet of the Total Force concept, which was developed by the secretary of defense in 1970–1972 when it became clear that AVF recruitment policies would be adopted. The concept calls for reserve forces, rather than draftees or volunteers, to be the primary source of personnel to augment the active forces in all future military emergencies.[1] Although this change may appear to reflect pre-Vietnam policy, two fundamental differences make the Total Force concept unique and make the mobilization capabilities of the army's reserve forces and of the Standby Selective Service System of great importance. First, the current size of the active army (which is some 185,000 personnel below the pre-Vietnam size) is justified on the grounds that the reserves will be able to provide combat-ready units and individuals on short notice. Second, because of the reduced size of the active

---

[1] In Pentagon plans, the concept of full national mobilization (as in 1940-1945) has been replaced by a much reduced call-up objective. Thus, in current discussions, the term "mobilization" refers to augmenting the active forces with all members and units of the reserve forces and sustaining this larger active duty force by a continuing flow of new enlistees or draftees. In total, the mobilized strength of the army would be about 1.6 million men and women.

1

army, the reserves have assumed a major contingency role, with commitments for deployment in the event of a mobilization that are nearly as demanding as those of the active army.

The fundamental problem with the current AVF manpower policies with regard to mobilization capability is that there simply are not enough men entering the Selected Reserve units and the individual reserve pools. Indeed, it is a paradox that the AVF decision prompted both the Total Force policy and the progressively worsening ability of the reserve forces and the supporting Standby Selective Service System to meet the commitments of the new policy.

In this study, it is hoped to clarify the extent and the significance of the current and projected mobilization manpower problems and to illuminate the range of possible corrective actions, their cost, and their political consequences.

The study consists of five chapters. The first chapter documents and assesses the mobilization responsibilities of the U.S. Army in the context of a conventional conflict between NATO and Warsaw Pact forces in Europe. The next three chapters analyze the current and projected problems within the Army Selected Reserve, the individual reserve pools, and the Standby Selective Service System. In each chapter, various corrective actions are proposed for management improvement. The final chapter discusses the importance of coordinating corrective policy changes with other mobilization factors, outlines several possible political compromises, and presents conclusions.

1

THE U.S. ARMY IN A CONVENTIONAL CONFRONTATION IN EUROPE

The military contingency that would make greatest demands on the United States Army's mobilization resources would be a sudden massive attack upon NATO forces in Central Europe. Such a confrontation probably would involve an intense conflict on land, and it might develop with only a brief period of warning (as opposed to the months or even years of warning before previous major wars). It might last only a few months, or combat might be very intense for the first few months and then drop off to a lingering war of attrition. In either case, the need for mobilization would be paramount. As explained by former Secretary of Defense Donald Rumsfeld:

> The force balance [between NATO and the Warsaw Pact] reaches an acceptable level of risk with the arrival of U.S. reinforcements, but only after a very critical period in the first few days when the force ratio could reach dangerously high levels. This clearly demonstrates both the necessity for U.S. reinforcements and the rapidity with which they must be able to deploy once the Pact's actions are known.[1]

Current Pentagon plans for providing these reinforcements call for the full participation of all Total Force units and individuals. In short, as an important Defense Department official explained to Congress, "The first months of intensive combat would have to be fought with the Active and Reserve component force structures that existed before the war started."[2] Thereafter, if the conflict were to

---

[1] Office of the U.S. Secretary of Defense, *A Report to Congress on U.S. Conventional Reinforcements for NATO* (Washington, D.C., 1976), p. VII-1.

[2] U.S. Congress, House of Representatives, Subcommittee on Investigations of the Committee on Armed Services, *Hearings on the Selective Service System,* January 21-26, 1976, p. 3.

extend beyond four to five months, the larger Total Force would be sustained through a flow of newly trained recruits provided by the reactivated Selective Service System.

The strategy of the United States for an extended conventional conflict in Europe between NATO and Warsaw Pact forces provides the justification for the Total Force structure and for the role of the army's reserve forces upon mobilization. Regardless of mobilization capability, however, the initial brunt of combat would be borne by the U.S. Seventh Army and other NATO on-site forces. The Seventh Army, comprising most of the more than 200,000 U.S. Army personnel in Europe, is deployed along the border in southern Germany. Its Fifth Corps and Seventh Corps, together with two West German corps and a Canadian mechanized battle group, make up NATO's Central Army Group, normally led by the commanding general of the Seventh Army. One of two army groups in the Central Region of NATO, the Central Army Group is responsible for the conventional defense of southern Germany, and its forces are concentrated to stop Warsaw Pact attacks through the Fulda Gap and Hof Corridor.

In a military emergency, the American forces would be rapidly augmented by dual-based units that serve in both Europe and the United States and by other units that have stockpiles of equipment and supplies in West Germany. At present such stockpiles are sufficient for an augmented force of about 2.3 divisions, the personnel of which would be airlifted to Europe in case of potential or actual conflict.[3] These initial reinforcements would be supplemented by sealifted divisions and support troops, including other active army troops (augmented by reserve "fillers"), and Army National Guard and Army Reserve combat and support units. As former Secretary of Defense James Schlesinger explained: "NATO, in an emergency, could well draw in something on the order of twelve or thirteen U.S. divisions not currently deployed in Europe."[4]

---

[3] Originally there was pre-positioned equipment for three division equivalents, but some of this equipment is being used for the two combat brigades added to the Seventh Army as a result of the Nunn amendment. See U.S. Congress, Senate, Committee on Armed Services, *Hearings on the FY 1976 Defense Budget* (Washington, D.C., 1975), p. 1142. Quick reinforcement of the Seventh Army by a limited number of airlifted troops from the continental United States is tested annually in the Reforger exercise. During the eighth Reforger, in 1976, for the first time, heavy equipment was deployed from the United States by ship to ports in Belgium and the Netherlands.

[4] U.S. Congress, House of Representatives, Appropriations Committee, *Department of Defense Appropriations for 1976* (Washington, D.C., 1975), Part I, p. 105.

4

Equipment Stockpiles

The effectiveness of the Seventh Army reinforcement immediately after mobilization would depend on the equipment stockpiles in Germany, for it would be impossible to transport heavy equipment quickly from the United States to Western Europe.

Despite the necessity for such stockpiles, in recent years they have been found to be in short supply and ill repair.[5] Furthermore, during the 1973 "Yom Kippur war" between Israel and the Arab states, the largest part of the army's tanks and heavy weapons stockpiled in Germany was shipped to Israel to replace armaments lost in combat. Three years later, the tanks and other heavy equipment had not been fully replaced in the stockpiles.[6] Indeed, in 1977 the Defense Department was still lamenting that "the degraded condition of these stocks would not only slow down the deployment of units dependent upon these stocks but would also tax strategic mobility assets in the early critical days of mobilization."[7]

Duration of Conventional Conflict

The U.S. Department of Defense does not appear to have made a firm or clear decision about the length of war it is prepared for in Europe, although there are indications that their strategic position is based on preparedness to fight for ninety days or more, as Morton H. Halperin, among others, has pointed out. His estimate of the ninety-day capability is founded on American planning and stockpiling of ammunition and equipment.[8]

A concern about the need for an even longer "sustaining" capability was expressed by a leading Defense Department official in 1976. Testifying before the Senate Armed Services Committee, William K. Brehm, the assistant secretary of defense for manpower and reserve

[5] U.S. Secretary of Defense, *FY 1977 Defense Report* (Washington, D.C., 1976), p. 203.

[6] General Michael S. Davison, who commanded the Seventh Army in Germany until his retirement in late 1975, spoke with me about the U.S. capability of providing reinforcements to Europe after having shipped stockpiled tanks and other heavy equipment to Israel. In General Davison's view, the lack of stockpiled tanks and heavy equipment in West Germany during 1973-1975 would have negated the tactical usefulness of reinforcements airlifted from the United States and would have significantly reduced NATO's response capability in a conventional conflict. See also, *A Report to Congress on U.S. Conventional Forces for NATO*, p. VIII-1.

[7] U.S. Department of Defense, "Deploying U.S. Forces to NATO," *Commanders Digest*, January 20, 1977, p. 7.

[8] Morton H. Halperin, *National Security Policy Making* (Lexington, Mass.: D. C. Heath, 1975), p. 160.

affairs, spoke at length about the shortage of manpower that the U. S. Army would have in Europe for the first seven months following a mobilization.[9]

Although the structure and capability of the U.S. armed forces are oriented toward a "long war," the forces of the European NATO members appear to be oriented more toward a shorter war. Exact figures are classified, but various observers have estimated that the European NATO members are not prepared for a ground war of much more than thirty days.[10] Indeed, one writer quoted a NATO official as admitting that his country's conventional forces had only a three days' supply of ammunition.[11] The European NATO forces would not abruptly withdraw from combat at the end of a thirty-day period, but the exhaustion of their supplies and ammunition would preclude their full involvement in the NATO defensive efforts. It therefore seems likely that a conventional conflict extending much beyond the thirty-day planning and supply limit of the European NATO members would become a struggle primarily between U.S. and Warsaw Pact forces. In this case, the disparity between the NATO and the Warsaw Pact forces would be so great that the conventional phase of the conflict would probably not last for any extended period.

Indeed, many experts believe that any war between NATO and Warsaw Pact forces would be very short. For example, Belgian General Robert Close, the commander of a NATO tank division, recently wrote that in a surprise attack on the Central Front the Warsaw Pact forces would be on the banks of the Rhine, in control of all of West Germany, within forty-eight hours. Other observers have echoed this view.[12]

---

9 U.S. Congress, Senate, Subcommittee on Manpower and Personnel of the Committee on Armed Services, Statement of William K. Brehm, assistant secretary of defense for manpower and reserve affairs, February 6, 1976.

10 See, for example, S. L. Canby and R. B. Rainey, *RAND Working Note WN-7078/1 ISA* (Santa Monica: RAND, October 1972), p. 6; and Leon Sloss, *NATO Reform: Prospects and Priorities*, Washington Papers of the Center for Strategic and International Studies (Beverly Hills, Calif.: Sage, 1975), p. 34.

11 Alain C. Enthoven and K. Wayne Smith, *How Much is Enough? Shaping the Defense Program 1961-1969* (New York: Harper & Row, 1971), p. 121.

12 See General R. Close, *L'Europe sans défense?—48 heures qui pourraient hanger la face du monde* (Paris: Henri Simonet, 1977). Another defender of a strategy that anticipates a Russian "lightning war" conventional attack has been the Mitre Corporation. See W. Gordon Welchman, "An Integrated Approach to the Defense of West Germany," *Journal of the RUSI*, March 1975. See also Kenneth Hunt, *The Alliance and Europe: Part II: Defence with Fewer Men*, Adelphi Papers No. 98 (London: International Institute for Strategic Studies, 1973), p. 3. Hunt quotes the former Commander in Chief, Allied Forces Central Europe, Graf von Kielmansegg, as saying that the Soviet forces, with some luck, could achieve a conquest of Germany up to the Rhine in three to four days.

Strategic Mobility

One of the key elements in providing U.S. reinforcements to the Central Front is this country's ability to transport military units to Europe by air and sea. Although government policies have supported its development since the early 1960s, U.S. intercontinental strategic air transport still exhibits shortcomings—despite being the world's best.[13] The more than 350 aircraft in the U.S. military fleet are an imposing resource. Many aircraft are grounded at any given moment for maintenance and service, however, and the combined capacity of all available aircraft would be sufficient to transport only a small portion of the massive reinforcements needed for a conventional conflict in Europe. According to an official assessment, the Military Airlift Command, with its C-141s as the troop carriers and its C-5s as the cargo carriers, would require about one week to transport a single army division, if most of the division's heavy equipment were already stockpiled in West Germany.[14] Thus, transporting the 2.3 divisions that either are dual-based or have stockpiled equipment would take approximately three weeks. And although the civilian air fleet of U.S. commercial carriers could also be mobilized for additional troop movements, the inability of the civilian aircraft to carry heavy equipment would limit their usefulness.

The U.S. sealift capability also raises serious questions. According to the Pentagon, the Military Sealift Command maintains only 27 dry cargo ships and 30 tankers, with another 139 mothballed dry

---

[13] A General Accounting Office study of the Military Airlift Command states that the airlift capacity is largely provided by the 77 C-5 and 276 C-141 jet transports of the Military Airlift Command and by the approximately 345 commercial jet airliners that could be made available in emergencies through the Civil Reserve Air Fleet. See General Accounting Office, *Airlift Operations of the Military Airlift Command During the 1973 Middle East War*, April 16, 1975. An attempt to double this airlift capacity has been made by the Department of Defense in recent budget requests. Congress, however, has not yet approved the funding for the additional aircraft.

[14] Robert C. Seamans, Jr., Secretary of the Air Force, "Planning the Total Force Concepts for the 1970s," *Air Force Magazine*, November 1970, p. 71. A more detailed analysis of the U.S. airlift capability was provided by the U.S. Army to the Library of Congress and is cited in Congressional Reference Service, Library of Congress, *United States/Soviet Military Balance—A Frame of Reference for Congress* (Washington, D.C., 1976), p. 30. The army's estimate stated that the planned move of the 82d Airborne Division to the Middle East in 1973 would have required one week if alert times had permitted prior preparation, longer if not. This move would have involved a somewhat smaller than normal U.S. division (about 11,000 men), a basic load of ammunition, and five days' supply of rations and fuel. The one-week time estimate for moving the first reinforcing division to Europe is repeated by authors of other works. See, for example, Sloss, *NATO Reform*, p. 40.

7

cargo ships controlled by the Maritime Administration.[15] To a large extent, therefore, use would have to be made of the 243 commercial dry cargo ships that carry the U.S. flag.[16] Many of these ships are poorly suited for military use, however, and would not be readily available as troop and military cargo carriers. (Since the adoption of the "realistic deterrence" policy, the United States has passed heavy sealift responsibilities to her NATO allies, who are expected to provide ships and related services in times of emergency.)

Although America's commercial air and sea resources could be mobilized with appropriate planning and a high degree of cooperation from the commercial owners, it is doubtful that such mobilization could be implemented quickly or could provide the capacity required for massive movements of troops, equipment, and supplies.

The success of the program of air and sea transport would depend also upon the preservation of reception facilities in Europe. Because many of these facilities are very close to the East German border, they are militarily vulnerable. Indeed, if the Warsaw Pact forces should manage to penetrate West German territory to any significant degree (and certainly if they should reach the Rhine in two to seven days, as some observers predict), the airfields in West Germany that receive and unload the large American jet transports would be in enemy hands or under hostile fire.[17] The seaports where ships unload U.S. reinforcements and supplies (such as those in Belgium and the Netherlands, as well as the main port, Bremerhaven, in northern Germany) also would be vulnerable, as would the 250-mile line of communication (LOC) between the ports and the current location of the Seventh Army in southern Germany.[18] Since no reinforcing units from the United States could arrive by air in less than several days and by sea in less than several weeks, the on-site NATO forces, together with

---

[15] U.S. Congress, Senate, hearings before the Subcommittee on Manpower and Personnel of the Committee on Armed Services, Statement of I. M. Greenberg, deputy assistant secretary of defense for manpower and reserve affairs, March 4, 1977, p. 22.

[16] Lawrence and Record cite interviews with Department of Navy sources that indicate that twenty to twenty-five ships would be needed to move one division to Europe and that the deployment would take twenty to twenty-three days. See Richard D. Lawrence and Jeffrey Record, *U.S. Force Structure in NATO—An Alternative* (Washington, D.C.: The Brookings Institution, 1974), p. 123.

[17] The main reception area for C-5s in West Germany has been Frankfurt's Rhein/Main airport, which is only 178 miles from the East German border.

[18] According to Lawrence and Record, *U.S. Force Structure in NATO*, p. 88, the United States does not intend to use the Bremerhaven LOC during wartime. Instead, the United States plans to relocate the LOC through ports in France or the Benelux countries. Lawrence and Record point out, however, that no funds, personnel, or facilities have been allocated to implement this plan.

quickly available reinforcements from West Germany and the other Continental NATO allies, would be required to defend the reception airfields and seaports for a significant length of time. Although alternative facilities could be located in France, away from the probable battle area, there is no assurance that France would allow American troops, equipment, and supplies to land. In all probability, failure of the NATO on-site forces to hold the West German airfields and the designated seaports would negate most of the potential benefit of reinforcements from the United States.

Conclusion

The first few days of a conventional conflict between NATO and Warsaw Pact forces on the European Central Front would be critical. If there were a long warning time, reinforcements from the United States could of course be very effective. In the event of a surprise attack by Warsaw Pact forces, however, the burden of defense would be on the on-site NATO forces. Furthermore, unless these on-site forces were able to contain the attacking divisions, the later availability of reinforcing units probably would become a moot issue.

It would not take long for the European NATO members to augment their units. For example, West Germany could activate reinforcements almost immediately in numbers large enough to bring its regular army units up to wartime strength and to provide additional home guard formations. Regular army personnel and reserves from the United Kingdom, Belgium, the Netherlands, and perhaps France also could be quickly added to the on-site forces in order to bring them up to full battle order.[19] In addition, although most of the U.S. reinforcements would of necessity not join their NATO allies in the defensive efforts until later, the initial wave of units airlifted from the United States would be in a position for combat within a few days following the decision to mobilize.

---

[19] Many NATO military commanders believe that the true reserves of NATO would be the French regular army, whose two divisions in Germany and three in France could provide much needed, immediately available ground combat strength. For a discussion of this point, see *A Conventional Strategy for the Central Front in NATO*, a report of a seminar held at the Royal United Services Institute on October 23, 1974 and March 26, 1975 (London: RUSI, 1975). For a detailed discussion of the military potential of the "surplus" reservists within the ranks of the NATO armed forces, see Kenneth Hunt, *The Alliance and Europe: Part II*, pp. 10, 31-33. Other analysts who support the greater use of European reserves in a NATO-Warsaw Pact conventional conflict include Alain Enthoven, "U.S. Forces in Europe: How Many? Doing What?" *Foreign Affairs*, vol. 53, no. 3 (April 1975), p. 520; and Lawrence and Record, *U.S. Force Structure in NATO*, pp. 103-109.

Nevertheless, many uncertainties remain concerning the employment of conventional forces by NATO and the Warsaw Pact countries in a European conflict. For example, little is known about how many Soviet troops are needed for internal security in satellite states. Nor is the reliability or availability of all Warsaw Pact and NATO forces certain, since some forces in the Soviet sphere might revolt and France and other NATO countries might stay neutral. Because the capability of both sides to augment and mobilize their forces is untested, it is relatively unknown, as are the readiness of reserve forces, in terms of training and equipment, and the ability of air, sea, and ground transport on both sides to move and then support large conventional forces and reinforcements. Relatively unknown, too, is the impact of a large variety of different weapons systems and logistic demands.

It is clear, therefore, that the many observers, commentators, and officials who offer hypotheses and predictions and defend specific scenarios do so within the limits of their best judgments. Although all these experts hope to define a reference point to use in determining strategy, tactics, and requirements for manpower, funding, and logistics, they cannot. No amount of research can hide the fact that a large number of variables and unknowns still remain, many of which are listed above.

The best possible contingency plan for NATO is therefore one that provides for all reasonable alternatives. Although it is unlikely that large numbers of reinforcements from the United States will be required, the availability of these forces would provide both a major bargaining asset in negotiations during times of crisis and an actual military capability in times of armed conflict. Thus, the current problems of shortfall in the army's Selected Reserve units and the individual reserve pools, as well as the diminished capability of the Selective Service System to provide emergency troops, should be of great concern to military and civilian leaders. Efforts have been initiated in Congress and in the Pentagon to assess the impact of the shortfalls and to explore possible corrective actions, but the problems remain unresolved. In the following three chapters, these issues are addressed.

2
THE SELECTED RESERVE: CURRENT PROBLEMS IN RECRUITMENT

The first major manpower problem caused by the U.S. decision to support its armed forces with volunteers is the inability of the army to maintain the minimum level of strength desired in its reserve forces—the Army National Guard and the Army Reserve. Because these units would be the nation's most ready resource for augmenting its active forces in the event of a NATO–Warsaw Pact conventional conflict, the progressive decrease in their strength has reduced the overall mobilization capability.

The vital role that the U.S. Army's reserve forces would be expected to play in a conflict in Europe can be seen by examining the army's requirements for personnel in the event of mobilization. According to the Defense Department, these requirements are:

	Mobilization day	Mobilization + 120 days
Combat-ready troops	660,000	1,525,000
Troops being trained	55,000	55,000
Casualty replacements	. . .	200,000
Total personnel	715,000	1,780,000 [1]

The active forces would provide the manpower initially required for mobilization, but the remaining 1,065,000 personnel would have to be provided by the reserve forces, through a reactivated Selective Service System, or through increased volunteer recruitment.

The Selected Reserve units in 1978 have a combined authorized strength of 602,400 (390,000 in the Army National Guard; 212,400

---

[1] A Report to Congress on U.S. Conventional Reinforcements for NATO, p. IX-3.

11

in the Army Reserve).[2] Many of the units are undermanned, however, and not all members are expected to report upon mobilization. Nevertheless, these reserve units would provide most of the additional manpower needed to bring the army to its wartime size.

Recruiting Problems and Shortfalls in Manpower

The ability of the Selected Reserve to meet its mobilization commitments has been severely curtailed by recruiting difficulties during the AVF years. The recruiting failures were particularly evident in fiscal years 1976 and 1977. For example, the Army National Guard started fiscal year 1976 with 395,000 personnel; by the end of fiscal year 1977, its size had shrunk to 355,000, or some 35,000 below the minimum authorized size.[3]

The same recruiting problems have occurred in the Army Reserve. Despite the fact that its lower limit was gradually reduced from 261,000 in 1973 to the 212,400 level of today, the Army Reserve still has been unable to achieve its desired strength. The recruiting shortfalls were most evident in fiscal year 1976, when 29,000 more men and women were discharged than enlisted. As a result, the year-end strength of the Army Reserve was 196,000. As of October 1977 this figure had further eroded to fewer than 190,000.[4]

The greatest recruiting shortfalls for both the Army National Guard and the Army Reserve occurred in the last two quarters of fiscal year 1976 and the second and third quarters of fiscal year 1977, and the situation is expected to worsen in 1978 and 1979 as the last of the draft-induced six-year enlistees complete their term of service. Indeed, the Department of Defense forecasts a shortfall in the Army Selected Reserve of more than 108,000 by the end of 1978.[5] This would be some 34,000 more than the shortfall of October 1977.

---

[2] The Army National Guard is oriented toward combat involvement, and it is composed of five infantry, two armored, and one mechanized divisions; twenty-one combat forces brigades or regiments; and assorted support units. The Army Reserve is oriented toward support and training. It is composed of the cadres of twelve training divisions, eight combat support brigades, and a variety of smaller units. For a detailed discussion of the reserve forces' organization, see Department of Defense, *Reserve Forces Manpower Requirements Report, FY 1976* (Washington, D.C., 1975), Appendixes A and B.

[3] Department of Defense, Office of Deputy Assistant Secretary of Defense for Reserve Affairs, "Reserve Forces Manpower Charts," September 30, 1977, Chart I-4.

[4] Ibid., Charts I-5, I-20, and I-21.

[5] Department of Defense, Office of the Assistant Secretary of Defense for Manpower and Reserve Affairs, *The All-Volunteer Force—Current Status and Prospects* (Washington, D.C., 1976), p. 13.

The shortfalls should be seen in relation to the mobilization requirements of the Army National Guard and Army Reserve. For example, although the 1977 shortfalls were reduced by lowering the required peacetime size of the National Guard from 400,000 to 390,000 and of the Army Reserve from 219,000 to 212,000, the level of strength required in the event of mobilization remains unchanged: the National Guard would require 430,000 personnel; the Army Reserve, 276,000.[6] Furthermore, some 5 percent of Army National Guard and Army Reserve unit members are not expected to be available in the event of mobilization. Thus, "fillers" would be needed both to replace these expected mobilization losses and to bring the unit strengths up to their mobilization levels. At the beginning of fiscal year 1976, the National Guard would have required 55,000 personnel from the individual reserve pools to reach the strength required for mobilization. At the end of fiscal year 1977, 93,000 fillers would have been needed.

The requirements for filler personnel for the Army Reserve are even larger. At the beginning of fiscal year 1976, the Army Reserve would have needed 63,000 fillers in order to reach the strength required for mobilization. By October 1977, more than 96,000 personnel would have been needed. Moreover, although it would not have been difficult to augment the National Guard and Army Reserve from the individual reserve pools when the draft was still in effect, the decision to support the armed forces with volunteers has caused major shortfalls in the pools (see next chapter). Thus, the increasing demands for filler personnel for the Selected Reserve units is compounding what is already a very serious problem.

AVF Reserve Enlistment Incentives

Recruiting for Selected Reserve unit vacancies when the draft was in effect was not a problem. Indeed, during the Vietnam War there were long lines of potential recruits, often prompted by pressures of the draft and the realization that since the reserve forces would not be activated en masse, service in the reserve would mean avoidance of combat. With the end of the war and the end of inductions, however, the waiting lists of applicants withered.

This change in the recruiting patterns for the Selected Reserve units was caused in great part by the failure of the Gates Commission, executive and legislative leaders, and military planners to consider the recruiting problems of the reserve forces in their detailed

---

[6] Data provided by Director, Force Mobilization, Office of Deputy Assistant Secretary of Defense for Reserve Affairs.

analyses and deliberations concerning the end of the draft and the achievement of an AVF. While they gave passing attention to the reserve forces, their emphasis was on providing the incentives needed to attract volunteers for the active forces so that inductions could be ended. In fact, until 1976–1977 no serious concern was expressed for the changing recruiting fortunes of the reserve forces, and even then little was done to help the reserves survive in the volunteer market.

The AVF has been sustained for more than four years by a series of major improvements in service pay and other benefits for the active forces, together with large reductions in the required sizes of the various forces. It also was necessary to pay bonuses for enlistments in combat arms and in other areas where there were shortages. While the general increases in service pay and other benefits were also extended to the reserve forces, enlistment bonuses were not authorized. Furthermore, the effect of the pay raises was not nearly as marked among reserve personnel as it was among active forces enlistees, because Selected Reserve members receive pay only for the few days each month when they are in training. At best, reserve pay is a supplementary income. But, in order to receive this income, young men have to commit themselves to an initial period of four months or more of active duty for training, follow-up attendance at weekly or monthly drills and summer camps, and a six-year eligibility for active service in the event of an emergency.

The recruiting programs of the army's reserve forces have not been totally unsuccessful. Particularly in the Army National Guard, select units have managed to maintain their strength and recruit reasonable numbers of young men and women with no prior service. An evaluation of these programs indicates that offering opportunities for membership in a respected unit, leadership, and community involvement are the primary recruiting tools, with financial incentives only secondary. Not surprisingly, most of the units that are successful at recruiting are located in small towns with long histories of community activity, and have linked the fortunes of the towns with the fortunes of their units. At the other end of the spectrum, almost all units in large metropolitan areas have had little success in recruiting persons with no prior service.

There are several management actions that, collectively, could reduce the shortfalls in the army's reserve forces. The policy changes that should be considered generally fall into one of two groups: (1) those designed to increase the supply of potential enlistees and (2) those designed to reduce the manpower requirements.

Increasing the Number of Recruits

At the Pentagon, thinking on ways to increase the number of qualified recruits with no prior service has emphasized providing more and better incentives. Such items as enlistment bonuses, educational assistance, and other new extras have been receiving prime attention.[7] While the adoption of these incentives would, of course, increase the number of recruits, the amounts that could be offered are currently limited by those paid to active duty enlistees and by the historic attitude of Congress and the American electorate that the levels of pay and special benefits for the reserve forces should be some proportion of the levels for the active forces. Thus, for example, if a man receives a $3,000 bonus for enlistment in the active forces' combat arms, a bonus for enlistment in the reserve forces' combat arms could not be justified at a level higher than $400–$900. In the view of most lawmakers, the disparity in amount would represent the practical differences in sacrifice and commitment between a full-time active forces rifleman and a part-time rifleman with a Selected Reserve unit. To make reserve enlistments more attractive, however, departure from such established proportional policies may be necessary.

Consideration also could be given to extending nonpay incentives. For example, in some states, the National Guard offers such additional benefits as state-provided tuition assistance, death gratuities, auto license tag discounts, and state tax benefits.[8] At the federal level, Pentagon officials could consider the value of providing reservists with post exchange (PX) privileges, life insurance, family medical and dental care, and some form of educational benefits. The G.I. bill educational benefits were one of the major recruiting tools for the active forces before the benefits were eliminated in 1976, but even during the Vietnam War, educational benefits were not awarded for reserve service.

The applicability to civilian employment of the training and the experience gained during military service remains one of the key selling points for enlistments in the reserve forces just as for the active forces. Indeed, the young men and women who enlist in the army's reserve forces for specific technical positions often receive ex-

---

[7] The Defense Department in 1977 attempted unsuccessfully to gain congressional authority to pay bonuses for enlistment into the reserve forces. The bonuses would have been $450 for a three-year enlistment and $900 for a six-year enlistment. If Congress had approved, the reserves would have used the bonus authority on a trial basis, with payments authorized only to select enlistees.

[8] Lt. Col. Sol Gordon and Capt. Clint Tennill, Jr., *1977 National Guard Almanac* (Washington, D.C.: Uniformed Services Almanac, 1977), pp. 44–60.

tensive training on active duty beyond the initial four months of basic training and skill orientation. For these individuals, the training obtained often is transferable to the civilian sector and results in better employment opportunities. Therefore, despite their overall inability to sustain required size, the army's reserve forces have had little difficulty in recruiting the bright young men and women needed for the more demanding and rewarding technical positions. Their problems have been with recruiting for combat arms, where there is a minimum of training relating to civilian employment. An argument can be made that the physical demands of combat arms assignments develop character, foster maturity, and bring out leadership abilities. In fact, the improvement in employability to be gained from training and experience in the combat arms is minimal. If training programs and on-the-job duties of combat arms enlistees were modified to include more experience related to civilian jobs, such enlistments would be more attractive.

There are several nonfinancial management actions that the Pentagon could take to increase the size of the recruitable pool and the number of enlistments of young persons with no prior service. First, the physical standards for enlistment could be lowered. This alternative might appear at first glance to be unacceptable, but there is evidence that physical entry standards for military service have been unnecessarily high—a luxury that was permissible during the draft years but is questionable in the limited marketplace of the AVF. The RAND Corporation, for example, conducted an extensive analysis of physical standards for enlistment and determined that these were higher than the entry standards for the armed forces of other advanced nations as well as for employment in entry-level jobs in the civilian sector.[9] Pointing out that the entry standards also were higher than those for retention in the services or for recall in the event of mobilization, the RAND study called for a 40 percent reduction in the rate of rejection for failure to meet the physical standards. Such a move would increase the number of qualified recruits by about 5 percent.

The second management action that could increase the supply of potential recruits for the reserve forces concerns the minimum mental qualifications for entry both into the armed services generally and into specific skill areas. The reserve forces already are recruiting a

[9] See David S. C. Chu et al., "Physical Standards in the All-Volunteer Force," RAND Report No. R-1347 (April 1974), p. 49. A report prepared in 1973 for the Senate Armed Services Committee also recommended a lowering of physical standards. See Martin Binkin and John D. Johnston, *All-Volunteer Armed Forces: Progress, Problems and Prospects* (Washington, D.C., 1973), p. 53.

16

large proportion of candidates who rank in the lowest 10 to 30 percent on the standard intelligence test they administer; yet even more such candidates could be enlisted. In addition, a great number of potential recruits do not meet current educational and intelligence standards for entry, and consideration should be given to a limited, experimental utilization of individuals from this group in the army's reserve forces.[10] A careful examination also should be conducted of the minimum intelligence standards for assignment to specific occupational areas, for the army may be providing overqualified personnel for certain occupations, with a resulting lowering of their effectiveness and an unnecessary restriction of the recruitable pool. Because some candidates refuse enlistment on the grounds that they cannot be assigned to desired skill areas, a lowering of the minimum entry standards for assignments to various skill or occupational areas would increase the number of enlistments of persons with no prior service. Again, however, the margin of improvement would be small, no more than 5 percent.

Another major management action that could increase the number of enlistees with no prior service concerns women. There has been a marked increase in the number of women recruited by the reserve forces during the AVF years, and the prospects for recruiting even more are very good. The recruiting records of Selected Reserve units have been spotty, however. While some units have maximized the use of women, others have avoided signing them on. Obviously, then, there should be opportunities in the latter units to increase the numbers of women recruits.

In summary, the size of the recruitable pool can be increased in only a limited amount without additional funds to offer incentives for enlistment. Each year the army's reserve forces must recruit some 170,000 individuals in order to replace losses and retain the size established for it by Congress. It is clear that the initiation of the non-financial management actions discussed above will not increase the number of recruits sufficiently to achieve this goal. It is also clear that additional men and women could be enlisted if reserve pay and

---

[10] The Department of Defense in the late 1960s conducted such an experimental program. Called "Operation 100,000," the program allowed the enlistment of up to 100,000 substandard recruits. Provided with special training programs, the recruits were assigned to regular service positions. This program was stopped after the election of Richard Nixon and the departure of Defense Secretary Robert S. McNamara. The views of knowledgeable Defense officials on the relative success of this program are mixed. Some point to the increased expense of the program and higher attrition rates of the participants as a mark of failure; others point to successful completion of their service by many enlistees in the program as a mark of success.

other incentives were increased. Thus, the problem faced by military and civilian leaders in terms of manning the Selected Reserve is little different from that which faced the Gates Commission in 1969–1970 when it tried to determine the amount of pay and other incentives necessary to attract enough additional personnel to the active forces to allow phasing out Selective Service inductions. Although the predictions of the Gates Commission on the costs of the AVF were later proved to be somewhat understated, its extensive research provided a cost model for debate and eventual decision making.[11] A similar research effort should be conducted on behalf of the reserve forces.

Reducing Recruiting Requirements

Several management actions could be taken to reduce the yearly recruiting requirements. First and foremost, the reserve forces could carefully determine their specific requirements for personnel with no prior service. In past years, the ebb and flow of available recruits generally determined how many veterans and how many men with no prior service were needed; with the guaranteed supply of draft-induced enlistees, there never was a problem of attracting sufficient numbers. Today, however, when recruitment is difficult and inducements costly, it becomes imperative that an exact determination of the recruiting requirements be made, including defining positions suitable for women. In short, to provide the basis for planning and possible corrective actions, the problem must be more carefully defined. With an exact blueprint of the recruiting needs in hand, it would be possible to take the one action that would significantly reduce the yearly recruitment target—reducing the size of the army's reserve forces by eliminating marginal or unnecessary units.[12] Point-

---

[11] See President's Commission on an All-Volunteer Armed Force, *Report* (Washington, D.C., 1970).

[12] The army's reserve forces reached their current configuration only after undergoing several major reorganizations within the last fifteen years. The first efforts were made by former Secretary of Defense Robert S. McNamara in the early 1960s. Rather than maintaining a large number of undermanned, undertrained, and underequipped reserve forces combat divisions (twenty-seven in the National Guard and ten in the Army Reserve), McNamara sought a smaller number of more responsive units for which more equipment and other resources would be available. In 1963 he was able to eliminate four National Guard and four Army Reserve divisions. This was followed in 1965 by the elimination of the remaining six Army Reserve combat divisions. The final major reorganization occurred in the late 1960s when the records of the few small reserve forces units that had been called to active duty in 1968 convinced Congress that fewer and smaller units would be more appropriate for future contingencies. As a result, the Army National Guard combat divisions were reduced from twenty-three to eight, and many smaller units were created.

ing out that many of the reserve forces units (particularly the Army Reserve) evolved out of World War II experience and would not be needed in a modern NATO war, critics such as Martin Binkin call for reductions of up to 150,000 billets.[13] Receiving particularly strong criticism are units that would play no role in a short-term conventional conflict between NATO and Warsaw Pact forces—such as those training for civil affairs, public information, and various other support functions. The army's reserve forces have begun efforts to identify marginal units that would not be needed in the event of a mobilization; they will be deactivated or converted to units for which there is a deployment requirement. But unanswered questions remain concerning the usefulness of many of the reserve forces units in a NATO–Warsaw Pact conventional war scenario. Thus, at the very least, an objective evaluation of current reserve forces capabilities in relation to that scenario should be conducted.

A better distribution of reserve units across the country could relieve some of the problems. For example, James Abellera determined that the National Guard strength in California is only 5.6 percent of the total Guard strength although almost 10 percent of the population resides in California. Conversely, the National Guard strength in Alabama represents approximately 4.5 percent of the total for all states; yet the population of Alabama is only 1.7 percent of the national total.[14] Thus, it would appear that future recruiting problems will be greater in areas like Alabama than in areas like California. If some units were relocated in order to take advantage of population shifts of recent years, there is no doubt that the Army Reserve recruiting problems would be diminished.

Conclusion

The recruiting problems of the Army Selected Reserve units cannot be considered in isolation but must be viewed in the context of the

---

Despite these structural improvements, the failure of the Johnson administration to call up the reserve forces en masse in 1965 and beyond threatened the reserve forces' credibility. Equipment was taken from them and sent to Vietnam, and additional equipment that they were scheduled to receive was withdrawn or diverted. For a more thorough discussion of the state of the army's reserve forces during the Vietnam War period, see *Annual Report of the Secretary of Defense on Reserve Forces, Fiscal Year 1972* (Washington, D.C., 1973).

[13] Martin Binkin, *U.S. Reserve Forces—The Problem of the Weekend Warrior* (Washington, D.C.: The Brookings Institution, 1974), p. 34.

[14] James W. Abellera, with assistance from Mimi Y. Dunham, "Prospects for Sustaining the Peacetime All-Volunteer Force, 1976-1985," *Defense Manpower Commission Staff Studies and Supporting Papers*, vol. 3 (Washington, D.C., 1976), p. 61.

Total Force. For example, since the recruiting of veterans by the reserve units is depleting the individual reserve pools to a crisis level, any solution for the Selected Reserve that sustains or even increases the use of veterans would only compound this problem. Furthermore, although the addition of incentives for reserve forces enlistees with no prior service would probably increase the number of such men and women, it probably would do so at the expense of the active forces' recruiting programs. Therefore, actions that would lessen or eliminate expected shortfalls in the Selected Reserve units must be analyzed in terms of their effect on the remainder of the Total Force.

The overriding factor that must be considered in all future efforts to resolve the Selected Reserve recruiting problem is the very limited number of prospective volunteers. With the end of the draft, large segments of the youth population ceased to be active candidates for enlistment because of their own economic and social priorities. Various Pentagon examinations of recruiting patterns have confirmed that when men and women who are in college, employed, or institutionalized, as well as those who fail to meet minimum entry standards, are subtracted from the pool of potential recruits, the pool is so depleted that the armed forces must sign up about one of every 2.2 available and qualified applicants to meet the requirements of the Total Force policy.[15] Furthermore, because of changing demographic patterns for youth, the recruiting prospects for the future are even less encouraging than they were in the first four years of the AVF.

Despite these discouraging predictions, the recruiting problems of the Selected Reserve units can be lessened and perhaps resolved through the implementation of the various management improvement actions discussed in this chapter. If these actions result in a resolution of the shortfall problems, then the nation will have been well served. If the problems are not fully resolved, then the nation will have to choose between a continuing shortfall in mobilization capability or a more drastic corrective action such as the institution of a Selective Service draft for the reserve forces.

---

[15] *The All-Volunteer Force—Current Status and Prospects*, p. 17.

3

INDIVIDUAL RESERVES: CRITICAL SHORTAGES IN THE EVENT OF MOBILIZATION

The second major manpower problem caused by the decision to support the armed forces with volunteers is the worsening inability of the individual reserve pools (the Individual Ready Reserve [IRR], the Standby Reserve, and the Retired Reserve) to meet the Total Force mobilization requirements.[1]

According to Pentagon plans, the army's mobilization requirement for trained personnel would be met by a call-up of the Selected Reserve units, augmented by men and women from the individual reserve pools. Personnel also would be needed to augment some active forces units and to provide casualty replacements. Although exact requirements are classified, a top Defense Department official told Congress in early 1976 that the demand for filler personnel would be approximately 51,000 for the active forces, a minimum of 120,000 for the Selected Reserve, and some 100,000 individual reservists to staff currently unmanned units that would be needed for the NATO contingency force structure. In addition, if the forces were deployed in the kind of intense combat expected in a NATO–Warsaw Pact confrontation, about 200,000 additional men would be needed to replace casualties during the four to five months before the army could train volunteers or draftees and assign them to combat units. In total, then, the Pentagon saw the need for some 471,000 trained fillers to supplement and support the Total Force structure.[2]

---

[1] The strength of the army IRR at the end of fiscal year 1972 (the last year of conscription) was 1,059,900. By fiscal year 1982, the strength level of the army IRR is expected to be only 119,000, or 11 percent of the 1972 strength. These data were furnished by the Department of Defense, Office of the Assistant Secretary of Defense for Manpower, Reserve Affairs, and Logistics.

[2] U.S. Congress, House of Representatives, Committee on Armed Services, *Hearings on the Selective Service System*, January 27-29, February 2-23, 1976, pp. 168-169.

21

Since then, the growing shortfalls in Selected Reserve units have increased the need for filler personnel. For example, by July 1976, only four to five months after the Pentagon's requirements were presented to Congress, the need for personnel to augment the Selected Reserve units had increased from a "minimum of 120,000" to 176,000; by October 1977, it had reached 189,000. If the additional predicted shortfall of some 34,000 by 1980 occurs, the need for filler personnel for the Selected Reserve would reach more than 220,000. When the number needed to fill out the active forces, staff currently unmanned units, and provide casualty replacements is added in the total army requirement for filler personnel would reach more than 570,000, which is 100,000 more than the 471,000 projected by the Defense Department in early 1976.

Just how many of these personnel could be provided by the individual reserve pools? The answer to this question is not easy to determine without the experience of a recent large-scale call-up.[3] Nevertheless, an examination of the mobilization yield rates developed by the Defense Department and the October 1977 strengths of the individual reserve pools makes it clear that at that time the supply was woefully short of the demands to meet the mobilization requirements. For example, there were some 188,000 men in the army's IRR pool. Given the Pentagon's 70 percent yield factor, a pool of this size would produce some 131,000 personnel upon mobilization. The Standby Reserve and other sources would increase the number of filler personnel by another 80,000–90,000. Thus, the combined returns from all the individual pools would not exceed some 220,000. Although the training output of 57,000 after mobilization and the appointment of an expected 20,000 civilians to military support positions would reduce the shortfall, approximately half the army's requirement for filler personnel would have been impossible to meet. By 1980, the situation will worsen. As noted in the previous chapter, the shortfalls in the Selected Reserve could increase by 34,000; in

---

[3] The numbers of reservists reporting quickly upon mobilization is not expected to be 100 percent. Planners within the Pentagon have estimated reporting percentages from the various categories, based on evaluations of the mobilizations of 1940, 1950, 1961, and 1968, with allowances for better management and control actions since then. Despite the fact that Standby and Retired Reserves have never been activated and that the United States has not fully mobilized since 1940, the Pentagon estimated that 95 percent of the Selected Reserve unit members, 70 percent of the IRR, 50 percent of the Standby Reserve, and 10 percent of the Retired Reserve would respond to a mobilization call. The percentages for both the Selected Reserve units members and IRR are higher than historical precedents. See Department of Defense, Secretary of Defense, *The Guard and Reserve in the Total Force*, unclassified portions of secret document (Washington, D.C., 1975), p. 11.

addition, the size of the individual reserve pools will shrink by substantial amounts. If mobilization should occur in 1980, the total shortfall could reach 400,000, a number representing more than a third of the reservists needed by the army and about a quarter of the army's overall requirement for mobilization manpower.

In determining the extent of the problem, the expected loss factor upon mobilization must also be taken into consideration. The army expects some 70 percent of the IRR to report; thus the size of the IRR must be some 30 percent higher than the actual mobilization requirement. This means that an IRR of somewhat more than 800,000 would have to be maintained in order to meet the 1980 requirement of 570,000 (an 800,000 IRR size would eliminate the necessity to call up standby and retired reservists). At present, the army expects the IRR pool in 1980 to contain some 142,000 men.[4] Thus, the shortfall in the IRR strength could be more than 650,000.

Reasons for Shortfalls

The continuing reductions in the size of the Individual Ready Reserve pool can be directly attributed to several factors that affect the flow of manpower as a result of the decision to support the armed forces totally with volunteers. Prior to the report of the Defense Manpower Commission in 1976, the Pentagon erroneously relied on draft-era data that overstated the number of men entering the IRR.[5] In determining these numbers, several factors affecting the flow of manpower must be considered. These are: the length of enlistment terms, attrition rates, the number of women enlistees (because women have not had reserve service obligations), the reenlistment rates, and the number of veterans who sign up for service with Selected Reserve units after completion of their active duty.

---

[4] Estimates on the future size of the IRR pool differ slightly. For example, an assistant secretary for defense has provided data to Congress that indicate an expected army IRR strength in 1980 and some 142,000; see U.S. Congress, House of Representatives, Committee on the Budget, *Hearings before the Task Force on National Security*, Statement of John P. White, assistant secretary of defense for manpower, reserve affairs, and logistics, 95th Congress, 1st session, July 13, 1977. Robert L. Goldich of the Library of Congress, however, estimates the IRR strength at 10,000 below the strength level cited by White; see Robert L. Goldich, "Military Manpower Policy and the All-Volunteer Force," Libarary of Congress, Congressional Research Service, June 28, 1977.

[5] Defense Manpower Commission, *Defense Manpower: The Keystone of National Security*, Report to the President and the Congress (Washington, D.C., April 1976), p. 421.

With a somewhat smaller active force size and with the trend toward longer enlistment terms, fewer men have been entering the army, and each year fewer of them have been completing their initial term of service. As more women have enlisted, the number of men has dropped even further. In addition, because more of the men completing their first term of service have been reenlisting, the number of men leaving active service has diminished. Furthermore, because more veterans have been signing up for duty with the Selected Reserve units, fewer men have been available for assignment to the IRR pool.[6] For example, in fiscal year 1976 the army enlisted some 195,000 personnel, 16,000 of whom were women. Of the 179,000 men, approximately two-thirds (or 120,000) are expected to complete their initial tours of duty. Some 30 percent of the 120,000, or 36,000, are expected to reenlist. The remainder, 84,000 men, should be released from active duty in 1979 and 1980.

In fiscal year 1976 the Army National Guard and the Army Reserve recruited more than 100,000 veterans—up from the 95,000 level of fiscal year 1975. Thus, unless dramatic changes are made in the overall flow patterns, most of the 84,000 men leaving active service in 1979 and 1980 will be recruited by the Selected Reserve units, and the number of men entering the IRR pool will be negligible.

Pentagon Proposals

The position of the Department of Defense on resolving the projected mobilization shortfall has been to discount the induction capabilities of the Selective Service System and the probable flow of volunteers coming forth in a national emergency and to concentrate instead on greater utilization of trained veterans. For example, the major two-year study of mobilization conducted by the Pentagon in 1974–1975 recommended that the current six-year service obligation of enlistees be extended so that all enlistees would be subject to re-call through their twenty-eighth year of age.[7] In practice, this would mean an extension of obligation for most young men of about four and one-

---

[6] Men who enlist in the active forces assume a six-year service obligation. The final, or sixth, year normally is spent in the Standby Reserve. Thus, the IRR is composed primarily of those who have completed three- or four-year active duty enlistments, do not opt for affiliation with a Selected Reserve unit, and have not yet completed five years of military service. Other members of the IRR include reservists who can no longer meet the commitments of service with the Selected Reserve and men who volunteer to stay in the IRR beyond their statutory commitment.

[7] *The Guard and Reserve in the Total Force*, p. 5.

half years. The secretary of defense accepted this recommendation and directed that legislation be prepared, but the proposal was never submitted to Congress.

Subsequently, Pentagon officials appeared to have reevaluated their position, and by 1976 they were calling for a change in re-call obligations that would result in each enlisted man being obligated for the five years following his discharge from active duty.[8] Since most men now are enlisting for three- or four-year terms, the adoption of this proposal would mean an average re-call extension of about two and one-half years.

Despite the very low annual flow of manpower into the IRR since institution of the AVF, the Pentagon has persisted in developing concepts of extended reserve re-calls. Yet, a close analysis of the number of men who would be available in the IRR under either of the Pentagon proposals clearly indicates that the proposals were not well thought out. There may be disagreement over exact numbers, but neither of the reserve service re-call proposals would do much to solve the problem of finding the more than 650,000 additional IRR members who would be needed in the event of mobilization. Furthermore, in view of the continuing recruiting problems for combat arms enlistments in the active forces, which is also the critical area for filler replacements, it should be recognized that an extension of the reserve re-call obligation through age twenty-eight (or for an average of two and one-half years) would discourage some potential combat arms enlistees from signing on. As a result, yet more special benefits, such as increased enlistment bonuses, could be necessary. Shortfalls could even occur. How bad the impact would be on the recruitment of active forces is hard to estimate, but there are so few additional candidates for combat arms enlistments that even a modest adverse impact could cause a recruiting crisis.

Management Improvement Actions

The current and projected shortfalls in the IRR can be reduced through a series of management improvement actions. Indeed, the Pentagon already has taken steps to amend the appropriate legislation in order to extend the six-year service obligation to women, who heretofore have not been subject to re-call.[9] Unfortunately, the move

---

[8] Committee on Armed Services, *Hearings on the Selective Service System*, pp. 172-173.

[9] Despite a shrinking IRR, the Pentagon waited until 1977 before requesting Congress to make legislative changes affecting the service obligation of women. The request was granted by Congress in mid-1977. See Public Law 95-79, section 803.

will not diminish the projected shortfalls in the IRR until women enlisting in 1978 and beyond complete their initial tours of active duty. Since women normally enlist for four-year terms, the first large segment of women should enter the IRR in 1982. From that point onward, the inclusion of women should increase the size of the IRR pool by about 8 percent. Although re-called women reservists would not fill the need of the combat arms or serve as replacements for casualties, they could be used to release male personnel for reassignment to combat units.

Another action to be considered is the reinstitution of two-year enlistments. Whereas enlistments of three years or longer provide the active forces with smaller training loads and greater efficiency, the longer enlistment term has a direct effect on the size of the IRR. Not only do the men and women who enlist for a longer term have less time remaining for IRR service following their release from active duty, but the longer enlistment term results in fewer new accessions. Regardless of whether the two-year enlistments were limited to combat arms or were implemented across the board for all occupational areas, however, the size of the IRR would not increase until the early 1980s when the new two-year enlistees would have completed their tours of active duty.

The armed services also could offer bonuses to selected, physically qualified individuals having needed skills, in return for a voluntary, but binding, contract extending the individual's IRR obligation for a period of several years or more. Furthermore, despite the acute mobilization shortages foreseen in the combat arms (armor, infantry, and medical corpsman skills represented 74 percent of the 1977 shortfalls), there are some surpluses within the army IRR pool in other skill areas, and many of these men could be used as combat arms replacements.[10] Indeed, men in all army occupational fields once had at least basic individual training as infantry riflemen; some had actual combat experience. Such surpluses exist in several occupations that lend themselves to relatively rapid conversion, for example, from military policemen to riflemen, artillerymen to mortarmen or tank gunners.

In other specialties where conversion is more difficult, a "double change" should be considered, for example, moving someone from administration to military police, thus freeing the latter for combat duty. The physical condition and capability of the individual must, of course, be considered. Nevertheless, there may be a sufficient

[10] Department of the Army, Office of the Deputy Chief of Staff for Personnel, *DCSPER 46 Report*, June 30, 1977.

number of qualified men in the specialties outside combat arms to help meet the requirements of combat arms mobilization.

There is also a potential for cross-service utilization of reservists, since the navy and the air force do not contemplate a great need for fillers but do have IRR pools. In some instances fairly direct transfers of occupational skills could be made. For example, a former air policeman should be readily usable as an army MP; certain supply and engineering jobs are similar enough for cross-branch transfers, as are those of cooks, clerks, medics, drivers, and many others. The other services' individual reservists could seldom fill the army's needs in the combat arms directly; however, a double switch in such instances in common specialties could be accomplished. For example, if the army's pool of truck drivers and clerks were depleted by their transfer to combat duty, drivers and clerks from other services could fill the army's need at least temporarily.

Another solution would be to enforce a ceiling on the number of men with prior service who could be recruited by Selected Reserve units. Such a move would force more veterans into the IRR and would help rather than hurt the Selected Reserve units in which there are some problems of imbalance between personnel with prior service and those without. The army also could set a ceiling on the number of first-term enlistees allowed to reenlist in the active forces. During the draft years, approximately 15 percent of those serving a first term reenlisted; now the rate is about 30 percent. A return to the 15 percent level would result in some 18,000 additional men each year leaving active service.

Collectively, these measures would significantly reduce the shortfall problem in the individual reserve pools. Many of the measures would create as many problems as they would solve, however. With the exception of using men not trained for combat in order to help meet the combat arms shortages, the other management actions would be costly and prompt serious recruiting problems. For example, if the army returned to two-year enlistments, the yearly recruiting quotas would increase by 50 percent. Admittedly, there would be a delay of two years before the additional recruiting burdens would be felt, but the tight recruiting market is not expected to change by then.

The same problems would occur if the enlistment of veterans in the Selected Reserve units were curtailed. Indeed, such a limitation would adversely affect the capability of Selected Reserve units to retain their strength levels and would compound their already great difficulties in meeting their recruiting objectives for personnel with no prior service.

In summary, there are no cheap or easy management improvement actions that could solve the IRR shortfall while retaining the AVF concept and keeping expenditures for personnel within reasonable limits. Yet, several of these actions could help reduce the problem, and their implementation should be seriously considered by army and congressional manpower experts.

The IRR Draft Alternative

A much more drastic and perhaps politically unacceptable solution to the shortfall in the individual reserve pools would be for Congress to legislate approval of a Selective Service draft for the IRR. Such a draft scheme could be implemented with minimum difficulty. For example, the current Selective Service policies concerning the lottery, selection, deferments, and exemptions could be applied to an IRR draft, under which the inductees would be required to serve for only a brief training period rather than for two years as previously.

Such an IRR draft would, of course, solve the problem of the projected IRR shortfall. The high probability of young men and women being inducted also would make them more interested in enlisting in the active forces or the Selected Reserve. The IRR draft scheme also would produce a younger, more viable IRR and would increase the number of trainees being prepared for deployment during the critical initial weeks following a mobilization decision. In addition, the IRR draft would exercise the Selective Service System, making it ready to function fully, quickly, and efficiently in the event of mobilization. On the other hand, the army would need authorization for considerably more military personnel and funds in order to accommodate both the IRR trainees and the necessary increases in the training staff.

As noted earlier, the army IRR could be short up to 650,000 personnel by 1980. Under the IRR draft scheme, this manpower could be provided by a variety of training and re-call obligation schemes. For example, 650,000 could be trained each year. Following four months of basic and advanced training, participants would be liable for immediate re-call, in the event of an emergency, for the following eight-month period. Although the induction each year of these youths would not come close to exhausting the potential pool of inductees (which would total more than three million men and women), the degree of inequity under the IRR draft scheme would be considerably less than under a return to Selective Service inductions for the active forces. Thus, the combination of a shorter training period, a limited period of re-call obligation, and a greater degree of participation of the nation's youth would make the IRR draft considerably more acceptable to Congress and the public than a return to the pre-Vietnam Selective Service policies.

Conclusion

The need for an effective, mobilization-ready individual reserve system is obvious. There are serious questions about the efficacy of the present system, and there is no doubt that the Individual Ready Reserve and the other individual reserve pools are the weakest links in the nation's mobilization resources. Not only are there severe shortages of manpower, but there are also very serious and unanswered questions about the reservists' usefulness and willingness to report.

The shortfalls in the individual reserve pools deserve serious attention from the nation's policy makers and other citizens. These men and women must recognize that the impact of the AVF decision is not limited to the active forces alone but extends to the other components of the Total Force. They must recognize that the reduced mobilization capabilities are causing severe national security problems and that immediate corrective actions are required. It is doubtful that these mobilization resources will be needed in the near future, but if a major conventional war were suddenly to erupt in Europe, the army's present individual reserve pools would be woefully unable to meet their mobilization responsibilities.

4

THE STANDBY SELECTIVE
SERVICE SYSTEM: A WASTED
MOBILIZATION RESOURCE

The third major mobilization problem resulting from the decision to
support the armed forces with volunteers is the erosion of the capability of the Selective Service System to resume inductions in the event
of a national emergency.

Since an All-Volunteer Force has never been considered adequate
in times of mobilization or greatly increased manpower demands, the
need for a standby draft system for use in emergencies has never
been in doubt. Rather, attention has been focused on the delivery
capability of the draft system—that is, the time it would take for the
standby draft to begin inducting large numbers of men. Further,
because the maintenance of the system's delivery capability is directly
related to the level of its on-going processing and staffing, attention
has also been focused on the appropriate level of funding for the
agency during peacetime.

The requirement for a standby draft, established by Congress in
1971, was based upon recommendations of the Gates Commission
and administration officials.[1] The key phrases of the legislative man-
date are: "The Selective Service System . . . shall . . . be maintained
as an active standby organization, with (1) a complete registration
and classification structure capable of immediate operation in the

---

[1] The Gates Commission made five recommendations for the implementation of
a standby draft system: (1) a register of all males who might be conscripted
when essential for national security; (2) a system for selection of inductees;
(3) specific procedures for the notification, examination, and induction of those
to be conscripted; (4) an organization to maintain the register and administer
the procedures for induction; and, (5) a standby draft system that could be activated only by resolution of Congress at the request of the President. See President's Commission on an All-Volunteer Armed Force, *Report*, p. 119.

event of a national emergency, and (2) personnel adequate to reinstitute immediately the full operation of the System."[2]

Mobilization Manpower Delivery Requirements

Specific mobilization delivery requirements for the standby draft were first defined in 1972–1973, when a National Security Council task force made recommendations based on the assumption that inductees would be needed in the event that a conventional conflict between the forces of NATO and the Warsaw Pact in Central Europe should last more than 120–150 days.

Utilizing the NATO conventional war scenario and the Total Force concept (call-up of Selected Reserve units, IRR, Standby Reserve, and Retired Reserve before beginning inductions), the Pentagon's Total Force Study Group in 1974–1975 again determined that a need for inductees would exist immediately following mobilization. As a result, the secretary of defense stated that the standby draft mechanism should retain the capability to commence inductions within 30 days after mobilization and to deliver a total of up to 500,000 men within 180 days after mobilization.[3] In January 1977 this requirement was raised to 650,000.[4] At the same time, the joint chiefs of staff stated their need for 100,000 trained inductees within 150 days of mobilization.[5] This requirement means that the standby draft must deliver the 100,000 inductees within 30–60 days following the decision to mobilize.

Reductions in Standby Draft Delivery Capabilities

The Standby Selective Service System retained the capability to meet the Pentagon's mobilization requirements during the first two years of the AVF. Indeed, with the end of the monthly induction calls in December 1972, the system remained an active agency of the federal government, with several continuing statutory duties, including the

---

[2] Section 10(h) of *The Military Selective Service Act of 1967* (Public Law 90-40), as amended by *The 1971 Amendments to the Military Selective Service Act* (Public Law 92-129).

[3] *The Guard and Reserve in the Total Force*, p. 32.

[4] U.S. Congress, House of Representatives, Committee on Armed Services, *Hearings on Military Posture and H.R. 5068*, 95th Congress, 1st session, part 5, February 3-23–March 16, 1977, p. 10.

[5] White, *Hearings before the Task Force on National Security*, Table R-5, "Standby Draft."

registration of each young man for possible induction, and his classi-fication and examination "as soon as practicable following his registration." [6]

A new concept of operations, scheduled for implementation in 1976, would have further cut funding for the system, local board processing, and administrative support and would have registered eighteen-year-olds once a year instead of on their birthdays. Even with these changes, the system would have been able to maintain its delivery capability. Unfortunately, however, resistance to once-a-year registration developed on political grounds, and the executive orders to implement the program were not issued. Since the old form of registration had been stopped in early 1975 in anticipation of the once-a-year program, the failure to authorize the new form resulted in the end of registration activities.[7]

When the end of registration removed most of the on-going processing from the local draft boards, funds for the Standby Selective Service System were cut to a level that required closing the local boards and their administrative offices. As a result, in the event of an emergency, the offices and local boards would have to be recon-stituted and a new registration program would have to be imple-mented. Because these tasks would be very time-consuming, the system in its present condition would be unable to meet the man-power requirements of the armed forces in the event of war.

Selective Service and the Standby Reserve

Members of the Standby Reserve (normally men in their sixth and final year of reserve service) are considered by mobilization planners to be immediately available, but federal law requires that the director of Selective Service determine the availability of each reservist. Thus, the change in the capability of the Standby Selective Service System that resulted from the reductions in its funds and staff has created a

---

[6] The Military Selective Service Act has not been repealed, but section 17(c), which is the induction authority, was allowed to expire. As a result, section 10(a) still requires the maintenance of a Selective Service organizational structure; section 3 requires the registration of young men; section 4(a) requires their classification and examination. The system also is responsible for determining the availability of members of the Standby Reserve, after they are ordered to active duty in a national emergency (Title 10, U.S. Code, section 672(a)(2).

[7] The failure of the Selective Service System to conduct either an on-going or a once-a-year registration would seem to be in violation of section 3 of the Military Selective Service Act. However, for the law to be enforced, "injured" parties would have to bring suit in federal court, and this is very unlikely.

basic conflict between the Pentagon's requirement that standby reservists be screened by Selective Service, alerted for active duty, and called up within thirty to forty-five days of a mobilization, on the one hand, and the ability of the system to perform the screening function within the desired time limits, on the other. Under contingency processing plans, the system would be able to screen standby reservists only after the reconstitution of the administrative and local board structure, a time-consuming process. Former Draft Director Byron Pepitone estimated that it would take about seventy days for the local boards to complete the screening of the standby reservists and that another thirty days would be required for leave to which soldiers are traditionally entitled before reporting for active duty.[8]

Legislative action removing the screening requirement or abolishing the Standby Reserve category by making standby reservists members of the IRR would end the current conflict. Since there is no pending legislation to accomplish these tasks, however, the reduced mobilization usefulness of the Standby Reserve compounds the already critical shortages in individual reserve manpower that were discussed in the preceding chapter.

Future Policy Choices

Five policy choices face political leaders and others concerned with the problems of the standby draft. They can choose any of the following options.

1. Repeal the draft law. One option would be to support congressional efforts to cancel authority for the standby draft through repeal of the draft law. Indeed, such a move has been continuously urged by a small minority of congressmen since the advent of the All-Volunteer Force. Such a development would allow the Defense Department or other interested agencies to redesign and modernize induction procedures and thus eliminate many of the problems that are inherent in the current somewhat antiquated Military Selective Service Act. Thus, there would be some advantage to a repeal of the draft law. To implement a modernized system, however, a lengthy legislative package would have to be passed, and it is doubtful that Congress would consider such "substitute" standby draft legislation unless the nation were faced with a military emergency. Even then, there would be no assurance that quick congressional approval would be obtained. Whereas restoring the expired induction authority in

---

[8] *Hearings on the Selective Service System*, p. 41.

the current legislation would require only a single yes or no vote, the passage of a complex new draft law would require time for congressional debate and consideration. As a result, there would be a risk of extending the current gap between the emergency induction capability of the Standby Selective Service System and the mobilization manpower requirements of the armed services.

2. *Continue the current system delivery capability.* Another policy option would be to support a continuation of the current "deep standby" status of funding and performance of the Selective Service System. If this option were elected, in the event of an emergency the system would be reconstituted along traditional lines—with state headquarters, local and appeal boards, the local boards having primary processing responsibility. The flow of inductees into army training centers would not commence until sometime between 70 and 135 days following the presidential decision to reactivate the system, with 100,000 inductees delivered some time between 115 and 150 days.[9]

The delivery capability still would meet the manpower requirements of the armed services, but no basic changes in the concept of Selective Service operations or in the Military Selective Service Act would be required. Furthermore, the system could be maintained at its current very low level of funding, and there would be the strong likelihood that further time-saving processing options would be

xperts believe that the emergency delivery time for the
' be less than the lowest estimate, and that the current
y" posture would not significantly affect the overall
preparedness of the armed forces. These manpower
o cite the following rationale: (1) there will be a long lead
/ mobilization (in excess of the approximately one month
: in current Pentagon contingency plans), and this long
ill allow the draft system to reactivate inductee processing

were estimated by former Selective Service Director Byron Pepitone
Director Robert E. Shuck. Appearing before Congress in 1976,
nated that the system could commence inductions at 110 days fol-
zation if men were inducted as part of the examination process;
they were given the traditional leave and travel time following
on and before their actual induction. In Pepitone's view, the
ed 150 days in which to deliver 100,000 inductees to Army train-
Hearings on the Selective Service System, p. 28. Shuck made his
lays in his budget submitted for fiscal year 1979. In Shuck's
delivery capability (with 100,000 inductees delivered by 155
ieved through administrative processing shortcuts. See Robert E.
ctor, Selective Service System, "Budget Estimates—FY 79,"

before the outbreak of hostilities; and (2) an emergency of the magnitude of a war between the NATO and the Warsaw Pact countries will attract sufficient additional volunteers that the need for a quick delivery capability from the Selective Service System will be greatly reduced or even eliminated.

During the draft years, the policy guidelines for mobilization consistently predicted a short period of warning. Thus, to claim that a longer period should now be considered in the case of the standby draft appears to be a major departure from previous policy, and a dangerous precedent. Furthermore, the restructuring of Selective Service local boards and administrative offices during a period of great crisis immediately preceding the outbreak of hostilities may not be politically possible.

In spite of the assumption of increased volunteerism during a crisis, the Vietnam War experience certainly illustrated that the United States can engage in military operations considered to be vital to national security without prompting a surge of volunteerism from young men and women. An attack by Warsaw Pact forces in Europe would probably be considered by many a greater threat to the United States than the Vietnamese civil war; nevertheless, it would be unrealistic to expect citizens to respond to a "call to the colors" as they did after Pearl Harbor. In sum, therefore, whereas the policy of continuation of the current system could provide a delivery capability greater than recent estimates, the uncertainties inherent in this option make it less desirable than other choices.

3. Adopt the system's proposal for major processing changes. Leaders also could support a new and somewhat revolutionary processing concept proposed by the Standby Selective Service System in 1977. The concept is designed to allow it to meet the mobilization requirements without a peacetime registration program or a large, on-going Selective Service operation.[10] The key element in the proposal would be the substitution of central computer processing of registrants for the traditional methods of inducting young men at local draft boards. Only those requesting deferment, exemption, conscientious objector status, or a reporting delay would be referred to local draft boards. Under this option, the legislative changes required to initiate computer processing would be developed but would not be presented to the Congress for consideration until an emergency, when the Congress also would be required to consider the restoration of the system's induction authority.

---

[10] See Selective Service System, "Budget Estimates—FY 79."

The key to success of this alternative would be quick approval by Congress of the changes required in the Military Selective Service Act. The proposal would not challenge the necessity for the reestablishment and maintenance of state headquarters and local draft boards, even though their workload would be reduced in most cases to only a few exceptions per month. It would, however, fundamentally change the historic role and responsibilities of the nation's local draft boards. For this reason, the willingness of the Congress to approve the legislative changes quickly should be viewed with some skepticism. Although the changes would probably be approved eventually, a delay of weeks or even months for debate and consideration could be expected if the emergency were less than a major direct attack on the United States. For example, if the President desired to build up the forces as a show of strength and resolve (as occurred in 1961 over the Berlin crisis), it is questionable whether fundamental changes in Selective Service practices would be quickly approved, particularly since these changes cancel what for many years has been the cornerstone of Selective Service operations—the jurisdiction of local draft boards over all young men from their respective areas.

4. *Adopt the wartime draft proposal of the Department of Defense.* The fourth policy choice would be for leaders to consider a similar but more revolutionary proposal for improving the system's delivery capability prepared by the Pentagon in 1976 and submitted to the White House for review.[11] Under this concept, exceptions would still be processed on a decentralized basis. But the more than 3,000 local draft boards, the appeal boards, and the 50 state headquarters would be replaced by 66 initial review panels (located at the armed forces' entrance and examining stations), 9 regional review panels, and a much reduced administrative support structure. The proposal also would limit registration after mobilization day to those needed to fulfill the required quota of fully processed inductees.

Although there is no doubt that the changes recommended by the Pentagon would significantly reduce delays in delivery time, the changes could not be implemented without major legislative action. Furthermore, the congressional action would have to change the traditional structure of state headquarters and local boards and the authority of the local boards for initiating deferment and exemption requests for individual registrants.[12] Under the Defense Department concept,

---

[11] See Office of the Assistant Secretary of Defense for Manpower and Reserve Affairs, "A Proposal for a Wartime Draft System," December 1976.

[12] Section 10(b)(3) of the Military Selective Service Act, reads: "Local boards . . . have the power within the respective jurisdictions of such local boards to

authority for initiating requests for deferment or exemption would be transferred to the individual registrants. Thus, if they did not request such status, consideration would not be given. (This concept is also fundamental to the system's proposal.) Critics concede that this change would allow much quicker processing in an emergency. They argue, however, that the local boards should retain their responsibilities to their communities and the families of registrants, and that this could be possible only if they retained authority to initiate classification actions.

Political power lies at the root of this controversy. Whereas very few discretionary judgments could be made by local draft boards under current limitations on deferment and exemptions, the situation was vastly different in World War I, World War II, and even during the Korean and Vietnam conflicts when the boards made many such judgments and, as a result, possessed real local political power. Much of the opposition to the proposals for reducing the scope of responsibilities of the nation's local draft boards must be attributed to the belief of many supporters of the traditional concept of a draft system that a major national emergency would require the restoration of many categories of deferment and exemption and the corollary restoration of the political powers of the local draft boards.

5. Return to peacetime registration or registration substitutes. Leaders also could consider the restoration of a peacetime registration program, together with the reestablishment of a limited capability for processing registrants. Under this option, the registration could be conducted by an enlarged Selective Service System or by some other government agency.

Registration by the Selective Service System is currently required by section 3 of the Military Selective Service Act. Thus, registration could be commenced with the issuance of an executive order. If the registration program were restored without reactivating the local boards, however, the delivery capability of the system would not be significantly improved. If both actions were taken, the system could once again meet the wartime manpower requirements of the armed services. Furthermore, an on-going registration program would keep the military service obligation of young men in the public eye and would prompt some additional service enlistments. Restoration of registration and limited processing would need to be enforced by the

---

hear and determine subject to the right of appeal to the appeal board herein authorized, all questions or claims with respect to inclusion for, exemption or deferment from, training and service under this title, of all individuals within the jurisdiction of such local boards."

Justice Department, because failure to register would violate the draft law, and an effective program would require that violators be prosecuted. Obviously, enforcement would be especially unpopular and perhaps politically impossible when men are not being inducted into the forces. Other federal agencies could conduct the registration program, but they too would face the enforcement problem.[13]

Conclusion

The requirement set by the Pentagon for inductees to be delivered during an emergency, as well as the gap between the current mobilization manpower requirements and the current and projected manpower of the Selected Reserve and the individual reserve pools justifies support for a Selective Service System capable of delivering a large flow of inductees, commencing within thirty to sixty days of a military crisis. Thus, it appears that the maintenance of the current "deep standby" posture—regardless of the possibilities for shortening the delay period—cannot be supported. Nor can a repeal of the draft law be defended. Instead, only those policy options should be considered that would reconcile the differences between the mobilization requirements and the Selective Service System's capability of meeting them. Consideration should be limited to (1) support of the system's proposal for a "processing by exception" procedure, (2) support for the Pentagon's wartime draft proposal, and (3) support for a restoration of peacetime registration and limited registrant processing.

No doubt this reconciliation would be achieved by a restoration of peacetime registration and limited processing. To be successful, however, the government would have to jail or fine nonregistrants, actions that should not be initiated unless absolutely necessary. Because either of the remaining two policy options would provide the required delivery capability without the necessity for peacetime registration, a strong argument cannot be made for a return to the pre-1975 registration program.

The implementation of the system's "processing by exception" proposal would of course provide the manpower required by the services. Quick congressional approval of the fundamental changes in processing and philosophy at the time of an emergency cannot be guaranteed, however, and it would be folly to count on an increased

---

[13] For a discussion of various alternative registration schemes, see Kenneth J. Coffey, "Implementing a Registration Program to Support National Service," background report to the Congressional Budget Office, National Security and International Affairs Division, November 1977.

flow of nonvolunteers when this hurdle would still have to be overcome. This rationale also should be applied to any argument for endorsing the Pentagon's wartime draft concept.

The most sensible option to endorse, therefore, would be the immediate submission to Congress of either the system's "processing by exception" proposal or the Pentagon's wartime draft concept. It is likely that strong objections would be raised in Congress to immediate approval of either of the proposals. But opposition to this full reform and modernization of the draft machinery would be less vocal during peacetime (when the machinery would not be needed) than during an emergency. If approved and implemented, either of these new concepts would provide the standby draft machinery to meet the wartime manpower requirements of the services. Conversely, if Congress should fail to approve the required legislative changes, there would be time to develop alternative courses of action.

5

CONCLUSION: A NEED FOR CAUTIOUS AND COORDINATED ACTION

The progressively worsening capability of the army's reserve forces and the Standby Selective Service System to provide the manpower required for mobilization is a major national security dilemma calling for corrective action. Before the approval of measures which could be either expensive or politically unpopular, however, it is imperative that the policy makers answer the several questions discussed in this chapter.

Have the mobilization manpower requirements been verified in light of the current shortfall in reserve resources? The determination by the army that 1.78 million personnel would be required upon mobilization must be subject to careful scrutiny. All subsequent judgments concerning the level of shortfalls and the goals of corrective actions depend on this figure, and policy makers must be sure that all these men and women are needed. The army's estimate of replacements needed for potential casualties should also be carefully analyzed. It is possible that Pentagon planners have set manpower requirements without a careful in-depth evaluation of needs—a common practice during the manpower-rich draft years. Even worse, the scenario could have been influenced by a predetermined decision to justify large numbers of mobilized reserves, thus providing a basis for continuing the current strength and high funding levels of the reserve forces. Although there is no evidence that the estimates of manpower requirements are biased, such determinations, by necessity, contain a great number of subjective judgments made by the planners and their leaders. In addition, the determinations of requirements usually lack the support of comprehensive research.

During the draft years, it was immaterial whether the requirements for mobilization manpower were precise, because the numbers of surplus reservists and the functioning Selective Service System gave Pentagon leaders the resources to adjust the level of the mobilized force easily. During these AVF years, however, such resources are not available. A price will have to be paid to bring the mobilization resources up to an acceptable level, and it is clearly in the interest of all Americans to limit this price to the minimum consistent with the maintenance of national security.

Are all 1.78 million men and women needed within the first 120 days following mobilization? The decision by the army that all 1.78 million men and women required upon mobilization would be needed almost immediately is a critical decision that should be subject to careful scrutiny. Newly trained conscripts or volunteers could be available 150 days following mobilization, with minimum additional cost and political opposition, but the insistence of the army that their units be filled 100 percent before this time nullifies the question of placing a major mobilization burden on newly trained volunteers or conscripts. In contrast, to provide the army with additional trained personnel immediately following mobilization, it would be necessary to increase the size of the army's reserve forces, an action that would require the expenditure of large sums or even the authorization of some form of compulsory service. Again, the requirement that all army units be filled 100 percent immediately following mobilization may be a legacy from the manpower-rich draft years. If so, and if it would be possible to provide some of the fillers required for army units beginning 150 days after mobilization, then substantial additional costs and probable political turmoil could be avoided.

Could the United States quickly transport army reinforcements to Europe by air and sea? The limitations of transport capabilities discussed in the first chapter raise the serious question of whether the United States possesses the resources to transport quickly the large number of army reinforcements and equipment that would be required in the event of a Total Force mobilization for a NATO–Warsaw Pact conventional confrontation in Europe. If, as is likely, the current capability for airlift and sealift is inadequate, it would be futile to spend great sums of money on incentives or to draft personnel to provide additional reinforcements who could not be quickly transported to the battlefields, or who, once there, could not be supported with the necessary amounts of food, ammunition, and other supplies. Instead, greater reliance could be placed on new conscripts or volunteers trained immediately *following* mobilization. In this way, the costs and political difficulties inherent in any program to increase the size of the army's reserve forces would be avoided. The key element in this issue is a reconciliation between the airlift and sealift capabilities and the mobilization plans for call-up. In the careful determination of manpower requirements for a European war, the availability of trained reinforcements should be matched to the transport and supply capabilities of the airlift and sealift commands.

Does the army possess the equipment and supplies necessary to deploy and support reinforcements quickly? The shortages and maintenance problems in the army's stockpiles of equipment in Europe (discussed in the first chapter), together with the continuing concern for the quantity and quality of equipment and supplies in the army's reserve forces, raise the serious question of whether the United States possesses the equipment and supply resources to support a fully mobilized Total Force. If the current levels of equipment and supplies would preclude the early commitment of army reinforcements to the European battlefield, again—it would be futile to spend great sums of money or to return to conscription to provide additional reinforcements who could not be properly equipped or supplied. To allow time for American industry to provide additional stocks, greater mobilization reliance could be placed on new conscripts and volunteers trained after mobilization. As in the issue of transportation resources, the key element in this issue is reconciliation of the army's equipment and supply capabilities and the mobilization call-up plans.

Is the Total Force concept viable? The quick availability of trained reservists for commitment to combat is the critical element in the Total Force concept. An examination of the three limited mobilizations that have occurred in the United States since World War II supports the contention that the expectations of the usefulness of the reservists who would be available—particularly "filler" personnel— are much higher than the real capability of the army's reserve forces. For example, the call-ups of 1950–1951 for the Korean War, which involved more than 139,000 members of the Army National Guard and 196,000 members of the Army Reserve, made only limited manpower immediately available for the active forces. Because of unexpected delays in readiness training and the necessity to receive and train large numbers of filler personnel, more than sixteen months elapsed before the first two National Guard divisions became operational. Much of the delay occurred because added training was needed to update the skills of the individual reservists, most of whom were World War II veterans who had not received any training since their demobilization in 1945. Furthermore, as Herman Boland pointed out, the army's records were not up-to-date, and many of the individual reservists were called with little or no forewarning.[1]

The second postwar mobilization occurred as a result of the so-called Berlin crisis. Men were called to active duty in the summer of 1961 and released some 10 months later. In total, more than 133,000 guardsmen and reservists were activated, including four Army National Guard combat divisions and one training division of the Army Reserve. As in 1950–1951, the army's planners underestimated the time required for these units to become operational. They had assumed that the reserves would take from three to five months to become ready for combat. In actuality, many of the units required five or six months beyond that. Although the Korean War had demonstrated that the key to quick combat availability for activated reserve units was a high level of unit training and a minimum requirement for filler personnel, the units activated for the Berlin crisis were still unprepared and had large demands for fillers. I. Heymont and E. W. McGregor estimated that when allowances were made for under-trained members of the Selected Reserve units, no activated unit had more than 48 percent of their billets filled with trained men who could be committed to combat on short notice.[2]

By 1968, the year of the very limited call-up for the Vietnam War, the leaders of the army's reserve forces, apparently having learned the lessons of the Korean and Berlin mobilizations, were maintaining units at manpower levels much nearer the strengths authorized for wartime. But only 82 percent of the wartime quota for Army Reserve units reported when activated, and 89 percent of the quota for National Guard units. As a result, individuals still had to be called to duty and absorbed, delaying training and deployment of their units. Expected to be combat-ready after eight-week refresher courses, the major units actually took some seven months, or more than three times the expected period.[3] Furthermore, according to an estimate by H. Boland, 17 percent of the reservists reporting for duty were totally unqualified for their assigned positions.[4]

Despite the limited scope of the three postwar mobilizations, they all raise serious questions about the estimates of time needed for

---

[1] Herman Boland, "The Reserves," *Studies Prepared for the President's Commission on an All-Volunteer Armed Force* (Washington, D.C., 1970), pp. IV-2-11, IV-2-12.

[2] I. Heymont and E. W. McGregor, *Review and Analysis of Recent Mobilizations and Deployments of U.S. Army Reserve Components* (Washington, D.C.: Research Analysis Corporation, 1972), pp. 4-7.

[3] Ibid., pp. 5-5 – 5-7.

[4] Boland, "The Reserves," pp. IV-2-22–IV-2-23.

refresher training in the event of mobilization and, even more significantly, about the usefulness of the fillers from the individual reserve pools. Had the units in the three mobilizations been able to be deployed without fillers, the time elapsed between their call-up and their commitment to combat or support roles would have been significantly reduced. Therefore, careful consideration should be given to eliminating, or greatly reducing, the current heavy reliance on the individual reserve pools for mobilization manpower. The recommended review of the army's mobilization manpower and time-phasing requirements, as well as the careful reconciliation of these determinations with the limitations of the army's ability to provide transport, equipment, and supplies, should somewhat reduce the mobilization demands for reserve fillers. But the army's need for such personnel is so large (521,000 in mid-1977), that it is doubtful whether all mobilization requirements for reserve fillers would be eliminated. Thus, consideration should be given to shifting some of the current mobilization burden from the individual reserve pools to the Selected Reserve units or even to the active army. Such shifts would, of course, require much greater expenditures to support the larger number of personnel. There also would be the problem of finding the additional recruits in an already very tight marketplace for volunteers. Yet, such a shift would guarantee the availability of the required number of mobilized personnel, a guarantee that cannot be offered under the current concept of filling out the active army and the Selected Reserve units with individuals from the reserve pools.

Political Compromises

The provision of additional personnel for the army (active, Selected Reserve, or IRR) may cost more in dollars and societal disruptions than the American electorate is willing to pay. Indeed, the expenditure of several billions of dollars for additional recruiting and enlistment incentives could be required. In addition, some form of compulsory service, such as a Selective Service draft for the IRR, may be necessary. As a result, it is likely that serious consideration will be given to compromising measures.

For example, leaders could agree that upon mobilization certain units would be manned by less than 100 percent of their wartime complements, with the reduction directly applied to the requirement for filler personnel. In making this assessment, the leaders would have to distinguish between units that must be filled quickly to 100 percent of wartime strength and those that could function at lower

45

levels while awaiting draftees to complete their number. In addition, an assessment could be made of the effectiveness of combat units that function at less than 100 percent strength for a while after suffering combat losses and receiving less than one-for-one replacements. The foregoing does not mean that the ideal objective should be any less than 100 percent, but, rather, that reassessment would distinguish different degrees of essentiality and provide a better basis for planning. Surely, not all units in the army force structure need to be 100 percent complete upon mobilization or shortly thereafter. While certain risks would be incurred even by this stratagem, distributing manpower shortages among units better able to sustain them would certainly minimize the effect of the shortfalls.

A second compromise would be for the nation to agree to accept the shortages of military manpower. If the need for mobilization does not materialize, or if mobilization occurs long enough before the outbreak of hostilities, the effect of the reserve forces shortfalls would be minimal. If there is little or no warning of war's outbreak, the reserves would in any case have little impact on the critical first weeks of fighting in Europe. Thereafter, however, if combat continues, a serious shortfall would jeopardize the capabilities of army forces for sustained conventional combat and lower the nuclear threshold accordingly, but U.S. strategic nuclear forces would not be affected.

In another compromise measure, a political judgment could be made that a NATO–Warsaw Pact war in Europe would develop only after a period of warning longer than that currently reflected in Pentagon mobilization plans. If this decision were made, it would allow a longer period for reserve retraining, the reconstruction of the Selective Service induction machinery, and the training of increased numbers of new conscripts and volunteers.

The warning time permitted by current Pentagon contingency plans (approximately one month) is based upon judgments that are, at best, subjective. Reasonable arguments can be made for either shorter or longer warning periods. Consequently, a reestimation of the expected warning time would not be a totally unacceptable political compromise, particularly if it would avoid the expenditure of additional billions and perhaps the reinstitution of conscription.

A Last Word

The mobilization manpower problems discussed in earlier chapters are not insignificant, and it is very much in the national interest for the citizenry to face the unpleasant task of taking corrective actions. The various management improvements and policy adjustments discussed earlier would reduce the scope of the problems, but they would not eliminate them. To accomplish this task, a return to Selective Service inductions, the adoption of a special IRR draft, or the expenditure of additional billions for new recruiting incentives, would be required.

In light of the very strong opposition to the draft exhibited during the latter years of the Vietnam War, a return to compulsory service in any form may not be a realistic political alternative, at least in the near future. Nor does it appear that the American electorate is willing to spend the additional billions that would be necessary to entice more men and women into enlisting in or extending their service in the army's reserve forces. Even if the additional monies were authorized, there is no guarantee that the expenditures would attract the required number of volunteers, for there are many competitors in the employment marketplace.

If these are correct conclusions, then the nation's lawmakers, in their eagerness to abandon the draft and adopt AVF recruitment policies, may have created even greater problems than were present during the draft years. Whereas Selective Service policies caused societal polarization with lasting damage, the AVF decision may have permanently lowered national defense mobilization capabilities. When the American people agreed to end the draft, they also agreed, probably unconsciously, to a progressive reduction in the nation's mobilization capabilities. If they remain opposed to the reinstitution of any form of compulsion or to the expenditure of additional billions for enlistment incentives, they are allowing a corollary increase in the possibility of both armed conflict between the members of NATO and of the Warsaw Pact and the use of nuclear weapons.

Cover and book design: Pat Taylor